ACQUA ALTA

Bedell Phillips

Acqua Alta
Copyright 2024 by Bedell Phillips

Published by Piscataqua Press
An imprint of RiverRun Bookstore
32 Daniel St., Portsmouth NH 03801
www.ppressbooks.com

ISBN: 9781958669297

Library of Congress Control Number: 2024945538

ACQUA ALTA

Bedell Phillips

Dedication

For Jason, Celeste, Nina, Johnny, Eliot, Torrey, Alice, and Summer

because they bring me joy

Acknowledgements

All gratitude to the literary journals publishing these poems. The author gratefully acknowledges the Best of the Net's nomination for "Thinking about the Violence." Bedell Phillips was honored in 2018 to receive the NANO Writers Award for Fiction for her novel *Around the Bend*. Chard deNiord, Tom Sleigh, and Rodney Jones are some but not all of the gifted and patient poets who have guided my work. Deep thanks to my interns, my readers, and my mentor, Tom Lux.

Poet's Notes

Invention of 'Thrums' as a poetic form has driven Bedell's work
in the last several years. Thrums are those threads left on the loom
once a tapestry is removed. They are the poem's last line. This form
brings the reader the zap, crux, or the essence, why I write.

Contents

Springtime Largesse

five story white pine lanky oak
hollandia flowering poppy
purple lilac bloomerang
weigela sonic bloom
tradescantia amethyst kiss
Caesar's brother siberian iris

our very own rapture

Interruption

the glory of the outdoors on the deck
the poet uses for the final book review

boisterous shriek and a response
back and forth between the couple

the female soft colors red beak
the male dark and soaring, leaves

with a stick in his mouth

A Momentous Spectacle

Rising from the shores of the Bay of Fundy, a boundless
sandpiper flock, ascends from the shore, up over
the water skyward and comes down again.

With dramatic swirling they create an ephemeral cloud of smoke.
Their black back coloration and white chest gives a pulsing
effect against the sky.

Low murmur of thousands of synchronized wingbeats and the soft
flight calls fill the ocean air.

Ancient cultures thought these patterns were a sign from the gods.
Today's scientists call this behavior murmuration.

Nature's greatest show

The Decline Dilemma

An older man
living in a small apartment
walks his dog
His glasses tucked
into his shirt
Gets home and they're gone

Next day meets a
young woman who
comes up and says
"Are these yours?"
Holding up his bifocals

Walking home seeing well he
goes into the bathroom
notices a white feather in his trashcan

the Spirit Guide

Sammy's Possession

The sun gleamed through the hazy morning. He was leaving grandma.
When he first had gotten there, he galloped directly into the backyard.

He ran behind the well-tended shrubs and perennials. She feared he'd
break them, twenty years of her work.

Then careened into the yard carrying a white pine tree branch. That tree
was one of the best, three stories high.

He drags it. During his gallop it broke in half. Laid on his back and
threw it up into the air. She was thrilled, called to her daughter,
"Look what Sammy's done. He's miraculous."

"Well Mom, you know he's a retriever." That night he hopped on the
Grandmother's bed. "No, no, Mom, he can't sleep on your bed. He's too
big and heavy."

Furtively, ears lowered, he walked over to her laundry basket, snarfed up
a tennis sock and sulked out into the hall.

That night all the kids, the grandma, the aunts and uncles, had butternut
pizza with herb mozzarella. Sammy walked around the edge of the dining
room table, black nose sniffing but took nothing.

Packing up the next day was chaotic. One of the kids left their towel on the
third floor. Another kid wanted a snack for the drive home. Black cargo
carrier on top of the car was finally full. They were ready to leave.

Days later, her daughter called, "Ah gee Mom, I'm so sorry." "What do
you mean my dear?" "Well you know Sammy is a retriever. He is trained
to take things. He loves you." "Yes, I know, of course he does."

Sammy took her sock and hid it in the car because it smelled like her.

Bubbleh

The dress had to be terrific
She bought it at Used But New to You

At home in her bedroom
She pulled the long tangerine fabric up over

her head, arms through the spaghetti straps
In the mirror she saw the midriff gap

I have to have it for my bubbleh
I'm so thrilled he got that girl!

I think long and orange is a good idea for the wedding
of the century that'll show that bitch Gracie

I'm gonna keep it
I've still got what it takes

That's why God invented a seamstress
There's one right in town

The seamstress greets her smiling
"Wow I bet this is for someone's wedding"

"Yes it's my nephew
dated her forever I almost had

to tell him to pop the question
but surprise he did it himself"

in the small dressing room with a full-length mirror
she again pulled the dress up tightly over her chest

5

arms through the spaghetti straps with silver ribbons
"Oh dear Lord, my breasts are hanging out"

We need some tucks to hold them in place
She called the seamstress "I really need your help"

She spoke with panic in her voice
"We cannot have the grandchildren see these nipples"

"Don't worry honey" answered the seamstress
"We got this."

We Can't Get There

leave Exeter and the Statue of Justice
holding a scale of balance

go down winding roads and open fields
past the tiny Newfields General Store

take a left the beautiful golf course and the Dance Hall,
gas station and then Dunkin Donuts

up the hill to Newmarket tall ancient factory building
river running right by its base

stone sign Welcome to Durham university town
tiny cafes and bookstores

in Dover many mini malls our scary eye surgeon search
continues but can't find it at all

preposterous beyond belief frustration
hunt for a white Eyesight sign and then

out of nowhere we found it

Backroad Phenomenon

late he comes down his two lane road to a dead stop
"What the fuck" strains to look sees no reason
there's nothing there

a girl halted her car in the opposing lane
transfixed looking at a lump in the road
inch-long fuzz minute shut eye
a newborn baby chipmunk

traffic backs up behind them

further up the road a rotted half tree trunk
right in the middle a dirty brown
cross-hatched plastic bucket brimming
with yellow marigolds and pink petunias

new life resurrection

Strength from Affliction

they decided to remove the waterfall
so the two rivers became white water
three trees all uprooted washed down
over the outcroppings

some had branches some had bark
but one was stripped smooth and clean
long cylindrical white with roots still attached

landed on the crag holding its power
roots separated from earth
like a father separating his violent boys

The Big Apple

Skyscrapers out the window
one with two colors
dark and light brick

Top floor arched windows
both first and last
all grey brick and
Bacchus bas relief
middle windows with
balconies dentils underneath

First with four windows lit
Middle has three windows lit
Last no lights at all
All across the street

Traffic, crowds and crime entirely below

Techy Trouble

he's on deadline
needs to send a copy
screen shared with his assistant

she's in San Francisco
he clicks on the zoom link
it comes up there's her gorgeous face

they work well together
he clicked on the right-hand share button
next had to upload to OneDrive

he has to share again click invite
he knew her email put it in
and shared again

as usual she got the email
he loved working with her
her editorial touch was perfection

then he goes to save it
pushed the save as button
and the whole article crashed

Technology Billing Problems

on deadline for the magazine
opened the emails early in the morning

an odd invoice came up
the tech company charged

his software provider
a new monthly fee

pulling up the software site
there was no customer service whatsoever

after thirty minutes changed the plan
and went onto the tech company's help line

still no help

Calamity

He got a great IT job working for a huge American insurance company. He had a terrific little space big enough for his computer and they gave him an ergonomic chair.

For several months a black thing moved across his computer screen from right to left. It was in the shape of a fedora. He finally decided he should see an eye doctor.

Made an appointment with a surgeon but it was not very near, way up in Somersworth, some little town he'd never heard of. According to Google maps it was near a famous university town. Whatever.

There were large yellow decals pressed into the office carpet. A sign instructed patients to follow the dots. The large circular lobby was edged with people sitting in chairs.

He waited forever in the surgical exam room. Then in walks this cute short pony-tailed girl. "Hi I'm Doctor Campbell. Nice to meet you." He was totally affected. His body was beginning to harden.

When he came out of anesthesia she walked in and spoke to him. "We got all of it out." "That's great." "Yes it is because it was wrapped around your optic nerve."

In the post-op the next day the nurse came in and said "I am going to remove your patch today." She started pulling, he put his hand up near his face. The tape felt tight. "Let's be careful." She got the patch off and dots of blood resulted. So alarming and his face stung.

He woke up the next morning. His face was beat red. Calling the surgeon was worthless. They never answer the phone. "This is fuckin' shit."

His dermatologist came to the rescue. "We can fix this. I'll put you on an antibiotic and Desonide cream. They are strong antibiotics, we'll look at your allergies. You've got to take it every 8 hours. I'm going to give you Clindamycin. It should have less impact on your stomach."

Upon leaving he realizes he must take eye drops every 4 hours 4 times a day, put that cream on his face 3 times a day, and take the antibiotic with food every 8 hours starting at 7 in the morning.

When he wakes up 3 days later he goes into his bathroom and urinates. Moving down the hall he feels an evacuating sensation and sees a long soft brown steaming cylinder.

"On my French rug"

Her Rib

The Cabo bus held 80 people all thirty-year-olds
going to the pre-wedding party.

The complex was huge and the hotel was far away.
She feared all her niece's friends would not memorize the bus number.

She stood up. "I am Alissa's aunt. Please memorize this bus number
so we all get back to the hotel safely."

At the front bus steps she turned too sharply then crashed
down the eight stairs past the handicapped chair.

Her brother leapt up caught her,
carried her all the way into the festivities.

Back at the hotel they wheeled through the vast lobby
to her breathtaking room. He ordered her food from the café.

Sitting there alone in pain she said to herself
It's alright honey the view is spectacular and the party tomorrow will be fabulous.

She received a text. "Are you in your room? I'd like to bring a friend
over to look at you. He's an ortho."

He walked in just like he was in his office told her how to sit.
He pressed his thumb carefully up and down her ribcage.

She reacted, "Not there but here." He repeated the motion.
She winced, "Yes you've got it."

"It's not broken," the orthopedist declared.
"Wow that's great news, thank you."

Limping out of her room she sat on her patio chair.
But hot from all day sun, it burned her leg.

What the hell can I do? Eat that salmon with
sautéed spinach I saw on the menu?

The wedding was on a huge outdoor tiled floor surrounded by palm trees,
she remembered as the wheelchair brought her to the plane home.

Seeing her front door calmed her soul, "Thanks for driving me from the airport.
Could you help me get my suitcase in the house?"

Following her through the door he lifted the suitcase onto the couch.
She sat down lonesome but proud of the journey.

She went to work the next day. A month later she couldn't get up
and every time she moved her left leg forward   excruciating pain.

Finding an ASPN at the hospital orthopedic center, he said "Have you had
any x-rays?" "No, but an ortho in Mexico stated nothing was broken."

"Well, we need x-rays and a radiologist to make that diagnosis."
He left the room and she waited there, alone and in pain again.

"It's right here. See that break in the ribs?" "Yes." "Also see that
white cloudy material next to the bone?" "Yup." "That means it's started to heal."

"Phew I'm real relieved to hear that." "You need something for the pain."
"I had taken some in Mexico." "Then you already know. You can go home."

He forgot to tell her how many pain pills are necessary now.

Statins A Medical Betrayal

His mom died in her sixties. Too early. The heart attack
made his dad so furious that he wanted to sue. All the kids
came up to talk him down. Then they decided they each
needed to know their exact cholesterol level.

So he went down to Big Boston Hospital. Got a female
doctor. She was cute. She tested him, got the numbers,
and suggested he go on a statin medication.

A year later he was twitching in the night. The neurologist
diagnosed him with RLS, an incurable disease.
Three years later another doctor told him,

"10% of the American population are allergic to statins."

A Search for a Good Man

he is the three pronged outlet
far right prong strong intellect
left one soaring soul
bottom round prong grounding

he brings the light takes away my darkness

The Vagina Is No Longer Empty

He looked like an Austrian hiker. She thought
he was German. "Hi," she said, "Is your wife
here?" "No wife. I single." Shining his blue
eyes right through her. The guide, hired by
the group, spoke perfect English, thank God.
Shanghai knocked her socks off. The skyscraper
observatory gave a stunning view of all the
river boats. Then she sat and watched the koi
beneath a teahouse. He was gone a long time.
She looked across the arched bridge. He was there.

8th Grade Dance

it was at the YMCA
called the spring fling

the DJ played
all the best rock 'n roll

then came the slow dances they
swayed back and forth sideways

he pulled her close
she didn't mind

at the next song
he again pulled her close

bent his head
around to her neck

sucked on her sweet earlobe
she felt him stirring

the music stopped
they stopped moving

she walked back to the chairs
he slowly followed

"I'm going to the john"
he found it down the hall

no one was there
he chose the last stall

shut the door
and jerked off

At Me and Johnny's Café

she liked that on the site he listed a goal of unconditional love
he said he preferred the phone to texts

she did not want him to see her car
because the internet is known for financial fraud

he's sitting on the little iron chair near the door frowning
she quickly walks towards him realizing her breasts are bouncing

she feels he's watching but can't do anything about it
she gives him a wiggly fingers hello

he shakes her hand with a firm handshake
she feels strong muscles in that hand

he holds the café door open
far enough so she doesn't trip

they took the food outside sat down
his bulging shoulder and pec muscles stirred

her hopes he looks at her and says
"Are you an author?"

"Yes I certainly am" He answers "I have a
good friend who's an author she's famous"

listening she draws a blank on the name In her salad
there were spinach leaves pine nuts messy dressing

and very long flat pieces of chicken *Oh shit*
I'm gonna spill all over my front how do I eat this?

"What are your books about? I'm curious" "Pretty much
everything -- politics relationships the environment Now

I'm working on a drug lord poem set in Miami I have him standing
on the corner the lace on his shirt showing his chest hair"

"I'm gonna get you a knife I'll be right back" returning he said
"They only had plastic so I made them wash this"

"Gosh that's really nice of you" "I was a chef in the Coast Guard
Knives were always an issue" they laughed

"One time we were in the Arctic Circle on this large cutter a crew of 375
There was a polar cyclone I was on the bridge next to the captain

Swirling water all white we couldn't see anything The captain
vomited into a bucket"

"Wow such an amazing story" she reacted
"I gotta go now"

At the Tiki Bar

the three-story banyan tree reaches to God's sky
huge 2 yard string holding dirty wicker pear-shaped cone
the small inside light shone dimly

long black hair, curled around her left breast
large sumptuous rose tat covering her right breast
a nasty detailed spider winds up her leg reaches the vagina

he slithered up to them his nipples showed through his light blue
rash guard shirt dirty toes peaked through OluKai Ohana sandals
hopped onto a stool, one leg raised

donker and 2 balls showing

Venice Flooding

Glorious Venice lives by the water. In the historic past, seawalls and jetties protected the city. Sudden floods called *acqua alta* flooded 80% of Venice in hours and covered the shallow inlets. Venetian flooding increased 5 inches per century.

Walter Mutti stayed inside his kiosk in spite of the flood's water damage. He finally went home and returned at 2 a.m. to save the newspapers. But it wasn't just wreckage, the kiosk was completely blown away. Weeks later a canal search found the kiosk in ruins filled with mud.

In the first two decades of the 21st century, 16 *acqua alta* events occurred. Ships must pass through a narrow inlet to enter the city. Flood defense is imperative.

To protect the city new flood barriers have been created. They are affixed to concrete beds on the bottom of the sea which when lifted up, slow flooding. Each gate has two huge hinges and the barriers are filled with water to weigh them down. Then the team injects compressed air raising the blockades to the surface. This combination halts the high tide.

To raise the barriers requires more than an hour. The water can rise 12 inches in one hour. 70 workers combine to check compressors, valves, gates, and the transmission system.

Venice needs an early warning system that predicts exactly when floods will arrive. For 40 years Georg Umgiesser, oceanographer, has conducted water event monitoring. From a platform ten miles out in the Adriatic Sea he records any significant changes.

His early detection system forecasts and prevents annihilation of the sacred city.

PFAS Water

"Chemicals dubbed 'forever chemicals' are prevalent and persistent in our environment countrywide" reports the U.S. Geological Survey. This causes a unique water-quality concern.

12,000 types of these chemicals known as PFAS are commonly found in consumer products such as food packaging, cosmetics, rainwear, clothing, furniture, and outdoor equipment. Furthermore, many PFAS are found in the blood of people and animals all over the world.

PFAS have been linked to cancer, low birth weight, thyroid disease. To further the research, Dr. Smalling, a head hydrologist, sent kits to volunteers. They collected water samples from their kitchen sinks at 117 locations including protected land, both residential and rural, where there were no known PFAS sources.

According to Michael Regan, administrator of the EPA, PFAS are "one of the most pressing health concerns in the modern world."

Cataclysm in Mesopotamia

At the confluence of the Tigris and Euphrates Rivers lays the Fertile Crescent known as the cradle of civilization.

Hashem Al-Kinani and his family have farmed 20 acres east of Baghdad, Iraq for generations. Rainfall is dwindling. The only water source comes from neighboring Iran. "The water flowing into Iraq has dropped 50% from the Euphrates River and roughly 33% from the Tigris River since major dam building began in the 70s," according to statistics from Iraq's water ministry.

Iraq's growth has added to the problem. Population soared from roughly 11.6 million in 1975 to more than 44 million as of July 30th, 2023.

The Middle East Regions are getting hotter faster than many other sections of the world. Estimates suggest a warming of 9 degrees Fahrenheit which would in the worst months of summer, create nearly unlivable conditions.

The once clear irrigation canal used by his farm is now nearly stagnant. The viscous, brownish-green water has a nauseating smell. Mr. Kinani stated, "We are irrigating with sewage water."

In many areas, water pumped from below the surface is too salty to drink, the result of dwindling water, agricultural runoff, and untreated waste. One farmer remarked, "Even my cows won't drink it." These depleted dirty rivers and waters are spreading an outbreak of cholera, typhoid and hepatitis A.

The head of the Najim tribe, Sheikh Muhammad Ajil Falghus, who was born in the village, said, "The land was good, the soil was good. Until the early 2000s, we grew wheat, barley, corn and clover.

Now we are living on the verge of life."

A Man on the Street in Miami

They were sitting on the school bus rented for their Garden Club road trip.
A straight haired graying fifty-five-year-old lady was reading the Miami Herald.
Next to her was her friend, a bleached blonde with curly crisp over-gelled hair,
wearing pink Lilly.

Straight haired remarks, "Gee, this story is reporting that drugs come up from
Colombia and are dropped off in Miami into motorcycle gas tanks. The bikes
drive to Laconia, NH for Bike Week. Then the drugs are shipped over
to Europe."

The two arthritic ladies hobble down the bus stairs. "You know there's a lot
of Colombians now in Miami. Watch out for your purse," the blonde said.
"Don't say that honey, it sounds a little harsh," answers her gray-haired friend.

A 4'10" man stands in front of the famous Spanish restaurant. His fighting
cock physique presses against the fabric of his white guayabera shirt.
Through the lace panel he sports a tangle of machismo chest hair that
protrudes. Reminding gray hair of her husband's pubes, she remarks,

"He looks like a Drug Lord to me."

Blackness

One cold November afternoon Exeter Academy was playing their archrival. So
many parents had come up to see the event. The kids and parents blanketed the
small town. There was a group of five kids all wearing sweatshirts and sweatpants.
Together they carried a sign saying, "We don't like that color."

All the kids were black

N.R.A.

Today many Americans realize mass shootings are now commonplace and that the N.R.A. has erected a firewall to safeguard gun control.

The New York Times reported on Sunday, July 30th, 2023, "Over decades, politics, money, and ideology altered gun culture, reframed the Second Amendment to embrace ever broader gun rights and opened the door to relentless marketing driven by fear rather than sport."

Although civilians own more than 400 million firearms, Americans still "are bitterly divided over what the right to bear arms should mean."

In 1975 Senator John D. Dingell Jr. began the ascendance of American gun culture. He was seated on both the N.R.A. Board of Directors and as a Michigan Congressional Representative. There he levied his high-powered position to both influence and lobby for a strong gun policy.

Throughout the last half century until his death, Mr. Dingell was aided by at least nine senators and representatives, both Republicans and Democrats. The New York Times disclosed that he transformed the N.R.A. to a lobbying juggernaut. This garnered elected officials' allegiance and derailed legislation behind the scenes. He deployed resources at every level to influence decision making. America's legal landscape was redefined.

The New York Times held documents at every hint of legislative threat proving these lawmakers served as leaders of the N.R.A., often prodding Congress to action. The N.R.A. accumulated unrivaled power.

In 1999 after the Columbine massacre, a N.R.A. executive gushed when Congress voted down gun restrictions, "We have strategic people in a place to make things happen. Thank you. Thank you."

Finally In Israel

They had escaped Nazism. She was born in Berlin, he in Poland.
Made it to the US, met in the Lower East Side.

Their son was a good student and they were so proud.
He had a girlfriend and he brought her home.

She was a schiza, pretty but not a Jew.

They, of course, had always wanted to see Israel.
At that night's dinner they acted different, all fidgety and excited.

"We have news," his mother giggled,
"we are going to Israel."

"Did you know we have an Israeli relative who is one of their generals?
We hope we can take her to dinner."

Their hotel concierge suggested a restaurant in the middle of a large boulevard.
"I know you're from the US, how would you feel about eating in the middle
of the road?" "Sounds like fun."

They all met at the recommended restaurant.
They all ordered drinks.

The Israeli General lept up from the table ran down
the center of Dizengoff Street, the main drag of Tel Aviv.

The schiza thought to herself *how could she be so rude as to
interrupt the father mid-sentence and then run down the middle of the street?*

Much later the general returned to the table. She looked different same face
but hard-lined. Sat down impenetrable. She spoke,

"The Hamas terrorists have firebombed a bus down the road. It was full of young children. I shot the perpetrators."

"Wow, that's amazing. How did you know?"

"I smelled the bomb."

Israel October 7, 2023

In 1948 the country Israel was founded as a sanctuary for the Jewish people due to 2,000 years of persecution and statelessness. Israelis expected to live peacefully in a combined future with the Palestinians.

An attack on October 7 crushed that combined identity expectation. 1,200 people were killed. The State of Israel could not protect themselves from the worst day of violence against Jews since the Holocaust.

Dorit Rabinyan, an Israeli novelist, said, "At that moment, our Israeli identity felt so crushed. It felt like 75 years of sovereignty of Israeliness, had – in a snap – disappeared."

Some Israelis, after all the atrocities, struggled to empathize with a Palestinian state. Yossi Klein Halevi, an author, in his book, *Letters to my Palestinian Neighbor*, sets out a vision for Arabs and Jews in the Middle East for a shared future.

He stated, "I spent years explaining the Israeli narrative and absorbing the Palestinian one – and I tried to find a space where both could live together, but I don't have that language right now."

An observant Jew, he stills prays for Palestinians, but more from duty than empathy.

Also by Bedell Phillips

Poetry

Recovery
Is There Life
Three Perch Swimming
Wolf Tail Glimmer
Where They Land
Thums & Tapestry
Edges of Waves

Fiction

Around the Bend

www.ingramcontent.com/pod-product-compliance
Lightning Source LLC
Chambersburg PA
CBHW022348040426
42449CB00006B/770